KNOWLEDGE ENCYCLOPEDIA
RENAISSANCE WORLD HISTORY

© Wonder House Books 2021

All rights reserved. No part of this book may be reproduced or transmitted in any form by any means, electronic or mechanical, including photocopying and recording, or by any information storage and retrieval system except as may be expressly permitted in writing by the publisher.

(An imprint of Prakash Books)

contact@wonderhousebooks.com

Disclaimer: The information contained in this encyclopedia has been collated with inputs from subject experts. All information contained herein is true to the best of the Publisher's knowledge. Maps are only indicative in nature.

ISBN : 9789354401329

Table of Contents

Renaissance	3
Quattrocento	4–5
The Cinquecento	6–7
The Italian Renaissance	8–9
The Italian Wars	10–11
Renaissance Art	12–13
Song and Verse	14–15
Sculpture	16–17
Architecture	18–19
Science and Technology	20–21
Exploration and Reformation	22–23
Islamic Eurasia	24
The Tsardom of Russia	25
Mughal India	26–27
Imperial China	28–29
The Unification of Japan	30–31
Word Check	32

RENAISSANCE

In Western Europe, the Middle Ages gradually came to an end in the 15th century. The period coincided with the rise of progressive philosophers, extraordinary artists and brilliant scientists and inventors. This period is known as the Renaissance. The term means 'rebirth'. It began in Italy, with a renewed interest in the knowledge of ancient Greece and Rome. Over the 16th and 17th centuries, it spread to the rest of Europe. The Renaissance coincided with the Age of Discovery, when Europeans discovered trade routes and lands, and colonised both the Old World and the New World! Great strides in ship-building, navigational tools and the use of gunpowder powered their advance. This was also the time when religious reformers tried to cleanse the Catholic Church of corruption, which led to the rise of the Protestant movement.

▼ *Early Renaissance blossomed under the patronage of the Medici family. Three of its most influential members are depicted in the fresco The Three Wise Men, painted by Benozzo Gozzoli around 1459. The young boy in the blue-gold hat riding a horse is a young Lorenzo Medici, later nicknamed Il Magnifico (the Magnificent)*

Quattrocento

The Italian term for the 15th century is Quattrocento. It marks the first phase of the Renaissance. Until then, **Constantinople** had been the centre of scholarship and culture. In 1453, when Constantinople was conquered by Turkish armies, many of its scholars fled to Italy. They brought **Classical** knowledge into cities like Florence, Rome, Milan and Venice, which led to the rise of the Renaissance. What was happening at this time in the rest of the world?

▶ Around 1401, Lorenzo Ghiberti (see pp. 18–19) won a commission to create a set of bronze doors for the Florence Baptistery. Historians mark this event as the start of the Renaissance. Ghiberti's doors remain one of the most valued treasures of the period

1419
Architect Brunelleschi designs the first famous Renaissance dome for the Florence Cathedral.

1420
After 115 years in Avignon, France, the Pope returns to Rome, bringing prestige and wealth back to the city.

1434
The Medici family become leaders of Florence.

1440
Oba Ewuare seizes power in West Africa's Benin City and turns it into the thriving and highly developed Benin Empire.

1443
Birth of the highly influential Renaissance architect, Leon Battista Alberti; King Sejong the Great of the Joseon Dynasty creates and publishes the Hangul, the Korean alphabet.

▶ In 1469, Lorenzo de Medici, the 'Magnificent', becomes First Citizen of Florence. His patronage of the city's artists and scholars leads to the high point of Florentine Renaissance

1486
Renaissance nobleman Pico della Mirandola publishes his 900 **treatises** on religion and philosophy. He is condemned by the Catholic Church but saved from **execution** by Lorenzo de Medici.

1490-92
Martin Behaim creates the Erdapfel, the oldest extant globe showing Earth.

1494
The firebrand priest Girolamo Savonarola becomes ruler of Florence and burns its treasures of art and literature in the Bonfire of Vanities.

1494–1559
The Italian Wars lead to the downfall of the Italian **city-states**. Artists and scholars leave to find safer places to live, taking the Renaissance to other parts of Europe.

◀ On 13 May 1497, Borgia Pope Alexander VI excommunicates Savonarola, who is hanged and burned the following year

◀ Behaim's globe, the Erdapfel

WORLD HISTORY | RENAISSANCE

- Birth of Leonardo da Vinci, the genius and **polymath** who is considered the defining Renaissance man.

▶ In 1495, Leonardo da Vinci painted his masterpiece, The Last Supper, on a wall at the Convent of Santa Maria delle Grazie

1440–69
Under Moctezuma I, the Aztecs become the dominant power in central America, historically called Mesoamerica.

1450
Johannes Gutenberg invents the printing press, making it easy for more people to acquire books and publish their ideas and beliefs.

▲ In 1454, Johannes Gutenberg published the Gutenberg Bible using the new printing press. Forty-nine copies of this valuable edition are still around

1452

1453
The Ottoman Empire seizes Constantinople, marking the start of the Ottoman Classical Age, which lasts until the death of Suleiman the Magnificent (1494–1566).

Birth of Guru Nanak, the founder of the Sikh religion in India.

1467–1615
Japan's Sengoku period is a time of violent civil war, ending in the country's unification.

1481
Spanish Inquisition begins its practice of *auto-da-fé*—public penance for condemned heretics, which includes burning them alive!

1471
Sixtus IV becomes Pope. He commissions major Renaissance projects such as the Sistine Chapel, but is also infamous for corruption and favouritism.

1470
Thomas Malory publishes *Le Morte d'Arthur*, the best-known tales of King Arthur to this day.

▶ In 1492, Boabdil, the last Muslim ruler in Spain, surrendered to Ferdinand and Isabella, bringing an end to the Spanish Reconquista

1469

1469
The marriage of Ferdinand II of Aragon and Isabella I of Castile leads to the unification of Spain. Devout Catholics, the royal couple begin the wars of Spanish Reconquista—to expel Jews and Muslims from Spain—and set up the horrific **Spanish Inquisition**.

The Cinquecento

The 16th century (Cinquecento) saw the rise of the Western world through naval conquest, trade and colonisation. Wars were now fought with gunpowder and cannon. Bloody conflicts between **Catholics** and **Protestants** dominated this era. Despite all this, science and art flourished, and the Renaissance spread across Europe. Elsewhere in the world, the Ottoman Empire reached its zenith, China ended its naval explorations, Japan suffered through the Warring States period, and India saw the rise of the Mughal Empire.

The powerful Safavid Dynasty begins unifying Iran, eventually turning it into one of the greatest empires of Islam.

◀ The Safavid Dynasty reached its height under Shah Abbas the Great (1571–1629), the empire's fifth and possibly its strongest ruler

1501

1503
Leonardo da Vinci begins work on the *Mona Lisa*, completing it three years later.

◀ The Mona Lisa, famous for her mysterious smile, is thought to be a portrait of Lisa del Giocondo, a noblewoman of the Gherardini family of Florence and Tuscany

c. 1505
Sultan Trenggana builds the first Muslim kingdom in Java called Demak.

1506
Following a series of drought, famine and plague catastrophes, over 2,000 **Marranos** (converted Jews) are killed and burned in Lisbon by Christians seeking God's mercy!

China's Ming Dynasty bans foreign trade and shuts all seaports in response to Wokou (pirate) wars.

1507
The first known smallpox **epidemic** of the **New World** devastates the indigenous people of a Caribbean island.

1600
The Battle of Sekigahara marks the end of Japan's Warring States (Sengoku) period and puts the military leader Tokugawa Ieyasu in power. Queen Elizabeth I allows the British East India Company to advance upon Asia.

1578
Mongol leader Altan Khan recognises Sonam Gyatso as a reincarnation of two previous lamas (teachers). He is given the title Dalai Lama—becoming the third incarnation of that line.

1558
Queen Elizabeth I is crowned at age 25, marking the start of the Elizabethan era—the golden age of English Renaissance.

1556–1605
Akbar the Great (born 1542) expands Mughal control over India with a series of conquests.

1550–51
The Valladolid Debate—on the human rights of Native Americans—is seen as the first moral debate in the history of European colonisation.

1548

▲ 'Wild men', shown on the facade (exterior) of the Colegio de San Gregorio, where the Valladolid Debate was held

WORLD HISTORY — RENAISSANCE

Copernicus publishes his theory of Heliocentrism; says 'the Sun lies at the centre of the solar system'.

◀ Statue of Copernicus with his model of Heliocentrism, in Poland

Italian diplomat Niccolo Machiavelli writes *The Prince*, a book of political philosophy for ambitious rulers.

▲ Statue of Niccolo Machiavelli, Renaissance historian, philosopher, politician, humanist and writer, at the Uffizi Gallery in Florence, Italy

1508–12 — Michelangelo paints his famous *Genesis* fresco on the Sistine Chapel ceiling.

▲ The fresco on the ceiling of the Sistine Chapel was commissioned by Pope Julius II, nicknamed the Warrior Pope

1512

1513

1516–17 — The Ottomans defeat the Mamluk Dynasty and acquire Egypt, Syria and Arabia.

1518 — The bizarre, month-long Dancing Plague is seen in Strasbourg, where hundreds of people dance without rest for days! Many die of heart attack, stroke or sheer exhaustion.

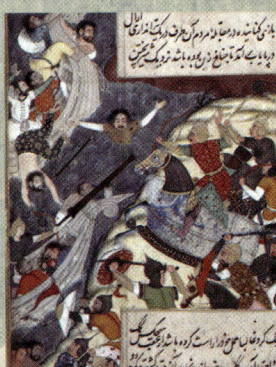

▶ Babur crossing the River Indus in the heat of battle, a painting commissioned by his grandson Akbar, c. 1589

The Turco-Mongol leader Babur defeats Ibrahim Lodi, Sultan of Delhi, in the First Battle of Panipat and establishes the Mughal Empire.

1547 — Ivan IV, nicknamed the Terrible, unifies Russia and is crowned its first tsar.

1531–32 — King Henry VIII breaks away from the Roman Catholic Church and becomes head of the Church of England.

1527 — The **Sack of Rome** by the troops of Charles V, Holy Roman Emperor, marks the end of the Italian Renaissance. The movement continues to spread outside Italy.

1526

1523 — The cocoa bean is introduced to Spain by explorer Hernán Cortés, and chocolate enters the global stage!

◀ Charles V on horseback, 1548, painted by the famous Venetian artist Titian

The Italian Renaissance

At the beginning of the Renaissance, Italy was divided into many city-states, each with its own government. The Kingdom of Naples in the south, Sicily, and the Papal States (with its capital in Rome) were in decline. In contrast, centres like Florence, Vienna, Genoa and Milan were flourishing, with a growing class of merchants and powerful noblemen. The Renaissance began in Florence under the patronage of an influential family of merchant-bankers called the Medicis.

The Spirit of Humanism

One of the best changes seen during the Renaissance was a change in general attitude, brought about by the philosophy of Humanism. This is a belief system —a way of thinking—that had existed in many forms throughout the world in ancient times. The Italian poet Petrarch (1304–74) discovered (and further developed) this philosophy through the letters of Cicero, an ancient Roman statesman. Humanism teaches that each person has the right to live with dignity; that all humans deserve access to knowledge and the means to break free from religious orthodoxy. It is a belief in a scientific and rational outlook. Through Humanism, people began to see that life was not just about fighting wars or working hard, but that it could be comfortable and enjoyable too.

▶ The front page (c. 1340) of one of Petrarch's manuscripts shows the imagined figure of the ancient Roman poet Virgil, who greatly inspired Petrarch

Renaissance Guilds

During the Middle Ages, people of specific trades came together to form professional groups called guilds. When the Great Plague struck in 1348, it halved the population of many city-states. People were plunged into poverty. At this time, certain guilds were able to bring stability in cities like Florence and Venice. Soon, they rose to power and became as wealthy as—in many cases, wealthier than—the nobility. Their patronage of art, literature, science and architecture became the driving force of the early Renaissance.

◀ *The Four Crowned Martyrs* is a Renaissance sculpture commissioned by the Guild of Stone and Woodworkers. It shows the guild's patron saints, who, legend says, were masons from ancient Roman times. Ordinary masons and woodworkers appear at the base of the sculpture

The Medici Influence

Followers of Humanism, the Medicis were wealthy bankers who encouraged art and science. Most famous among them was Lorenzo (1449–92). As the First Citizen of the Republic of Florence, he turned the city into a spectacular centre of Renaissance. His example was followed across Italy. The Sforzas of Milan, the Montefeltro dukes of Urbino, the Orsinis and Colonnas of Rome and the Bentivoglios of Bologna were some of the other patrons of the Renaissance. Their families produced some of the most colourful cardinals, popes and **condottieri** in Italian history.

▶ *Painted by the brilliant Boticelli (1445–1510), the Madonna del Magnificat shows the poet and political adviser Lucrezia with her children. A young Lorenzo is holding the inkpot*

The Renaissance Leaves Italy

The end of Italy's Renaissance came slowly as new east-west trade routes were discovered that left out Italian port-cities. Religious fervour rose again when the monk Girolamo Savonarola took control of Florence over 1494–98. This culminated in the horrific Bonfire of Vanities—the public burning of great works of scholarship, poetry and art. In the same period, Italy also faced a series of foreign invasions. In 1527, the armies of Charles V, Holy Roman Emperor, looted and destroyed Rome. The Sack of Rome greatly reduced Papal power. Many Renaissance masters left to find patrons in other cities. Thus, the Renaissance spread out to Europe.

▲ *A Majolica (tin-glazed earthenware) plate from c. 1540 shows a scene from the 1527 Sack of Rome*

▲ *Girolamo Savonarola by Renaissance artist Fra Bartolomeo, c. 1498*

In Real Life

The Vatican City is the world's smallest, fully independent nation. Set within medieval and Renaissance walls, it is also the only country to be a full UNESCO World Heritage Site.

▲ *The iconic St Peter's Basilica at the heart of the Vatican City*

◀ *The Medici family gave France two of its most influential queens. Catherine de'Medici (1519–89), on the far left, married Henry II of France and gave birth to three of its later kings—Francis II, Charles IX and Henry III. Marie de'Medici (1575–1642) married Henry IV of France and ruled the country after his death with great political acumen. She was immortalised by the genius Rubens in a series of 24 amazing paintings*

The Italian Wars

During the Renaissance, small feudal princedoms in Western Europe fused together to form great competing monarchies. At the end of the 15th century, the most notable were Spain, France, England and the Holy Roman Empire. For the next 150 years, they quarrelled, made friends, and then quarrelled again. The Italian Wars (1494–1559) were a series of battles they fought to control the independent city-states of Italy.

French Ambitions

In 1494–1495, King Charles VIII of France invaded Italy. Assisted by Ludovico Sforza, the Tyrant of Milan, he seized Naples. In response, Venice, Mantua and Rome allied with Spain and the Holy Roman Emperor to drive him away. In 1499, Charles VIII's successor, Louis XII, captured northwest Italy, including Milan and Genoa. Louis then schemed with Ferdinand V of Spain to conquer Naples and divide it between themselves. But they couldn't agree on how to split it fairly. By 1502, the French and Spanish parties were in open war! Louis was eventually forced to sign the Treaty of Blois (1504–1505). He kept Milan and Genoa, but promised to hand over Naples to Spain.

▲ The courageous Chevalier de Bayard fought in the Battle of Garigliano (1503) and ensured the safe retreat of the French army by defending a bridge against the enemy

▲ Kings of France: Charles VIII (1470–1498) and Louis XII (1462–1515)

Incredible Individuals

The marriage of Ferdinand of Aragon and Isabella of Castile in 1469 led to a unified Spain that grew rapidly through trade, conquest and colonisation. By the early 16th century, their grandson Charles V, Holy Roman Emperor, ruled the most powerful empire in Europe and the New World. He was also head of the rising House of Habsburgs, who would rule most of Europe in the coming centuries.

▶ Marriage portrait of Ferdinand and Isabella

The Republic of Venice

Venice tried to extend its territories by exploiting the tensions between the mighty empires. But in 1509, it was crushed by a new alliance of France. It was Spain, the Holy Roman Empire and Pope Julius II. Shortly after, the Pope made peace with Venice. They formed a Holy League with other powers to expel France from Milan. In 1513, Swiss mercenaries of the League routed the French at Novara. They took control of Lombardy (northern Italy) and held it until 1515, when Louis's successor, Francis I, defeated them. The peace of Noyon (1516) gave Milan back to France, while Naples remained with Spain.

The Battle of Pavia

After Charles V became King of Spain (in 1516) and then Holy Roman Emperor (1519, in Germany), he and his allies expelled the French from Milan in 1521. Francis I, King of France, made new attempts to recapture the city, but was defeated, and captured in 1525 during the Battle of Pavia. France was compelled to sign the Treaty of Madrid (1526), renouncing its Italian claims and even giving up Burgundy.

▲ Maximilian I (1459–1519), Holy Roman Emperor, in his armour; painted by Peter Paul Rubens nearly 100 years after the monarch's death

The Sack of Rome

As soon as he was released, Francis I broke the treaty. He formed the League of Cognac with Venice, Florence, Pope Clement VII and Henry VIII of England. Outraged, Charles V sent his troops to punish the Pope. They sacked Rome for a full week in May 1527.

▲ At the Battle of Pavia, the Imperial army (under statesman Charles de Lannoy and commander of the Pavia garrison, Antonio de Leyva) attacked the French army (under the command of Francis I) on the hunting grounds of Mirabello, outside the city walls. Within four hours, the French were defeated. Their king was captured and imprisoned

▲ The Sack of Rome, by Dutch Golden-Age painter Johannes Lingelbach

Habsburg Victories

The French did not meet with lasting success. The flourishing port of Genoa, with its naval fleet, sided with Charles V in 1528. The emperor also restored power to the Medicis, making them princes of Florence. In 1529, France signed the Treaty of Cambrai, once more giving up on Italy. Two later French wars (in 1542–1544 and 1556–1557) also ended in failure. Francis died in 1547, after signing a third treaty, at Crepy, renouncing Naples. His successor Henry II did not fare much better against the Habsburg emperor.

▶ Charles V (1500–1558) and Philip II (1527–1598), both portraits by Renaissance master-painter Titian

Renaissance Art

During the Middle Ages, art in Western Europe was restricted to Christian subjects and icons. The images were flat and evenly coloured. A great deal of Renaissance art was also religious. But it also explored Classical mythology and daily life. Most importantly, for the first time, art began to look three-dimensional and realistic. The architect Brunelleschi (1377–1446) described the rules of **perspective,** which helped create amazing compositions. Artists developed techniques like **sfumato** and **chiaroscuro**, which gave paintings soft lines, delicate shading and compelling light-and-shadow effects. Oil painting and a new type of fast-drying fresco came to the forefront at this time.

▲ In 1486, Sandro Boticelli completed The Birth of Venus, a masterpiece of Florentine Renaissance. Under the influence of Savonarola, Boticelli burnt some of his precious paintings in the Bonfire of Vanities (see p. 9)

▲ Judith Beheading Holofernes is a Biblical story painted over 1599–1602 by Caravaggio using a technique called chiaroscuro, which is a way of creating bold contrasts between light and dark

The Renaissance Triumvirate

The three most famous masters of the Italian Renaissance are Leonardo da Vinci (1452–1519), Michelangelo (1475–1564) and Raphael (1483–1520). They studied human anatomy so they could accurately portray movement of muscle, bone and expression. Da Vinci dissected some 30 corpses and made 13,000 pages worth of drawings on animals, nature, humans, and even on scientific inventions, war machines and city defences.

▲ The School of Athens, an amazing fresco by Raphael, depicts Classical scholars with the faces of Renaissance geniuses. The central figure with the flowing beard is the great Greek philosopher Plato, modelled after Leonardo da Vinci. Michelangelo is drawn as the Greek philosopher Heraclitus sitting alone, brooding, in the foreground (both men were loners)

▲ Da Vinci's Mona Lisa was created using sfumato, a technique that uses varying shades of colours to build up an image (no lines are drawn)

WORLD HISTORY | RENAISSANCE | 13

▲ Michelangelo imbued his paintings with muscular power and contained turbulence, as seen in his incredible Genesis fresco, The Creation of Adam, on the Sistine Chapel ceiling in Rome

Flemish and Dutch Art

Northern painters showed a great deal of interest in nature and real life. The works of Pieter Brueghel the Elder (c. 1525–1559) capture the magic of the age in vivid colours and a multitude of figures. A unique artist of this time was Hieronymous Bosch (1450–1516), who painted complex, dreamlike canvasses that often evoked fear and confusion.

▲ The Peasant Dance by Pieter Brueghel the Elder

Titian

The greatest painter of Renaissance Venice was Tiziano Vecellio (c.1488–1576), known to English-speakers as Titian. He developed a system of colour painting that had three main guidelines—limit the number of colours, choose the richest and purest form of those colours, and create a simple harmony with colour. This contrasted with the established Renaissance practice of using a great variety of colours.

▲ Bosch's imaginative Hell, a panel from his triptych, The Garden of Earthly Delights

▲ Titian's amazingly rich colour work in The Assumption of the Virgin (1516–1518) caused a sensation when it was first unveiled

▲ Tintoretto's luminous masterpiece, Presentation of the Virgin in the Temple (1550–1553)

▲ El Greco's The Burial of the Count of Orgaz (1586–1588) is a harmony of earthly and heavenly figures in saturated hues and brilliant contrasts

Song and Verse

With the invention of the printing press, the ideas of Humanist scholars and Protestant reformers filled books and pamphlets, marking a new age of literature. Playwrights and poets reached a wider audience, since their most popular works weren't limited to performances, but could be printed and distributed. Most importantly, writing was no longer limited to 'scholarly' languages like Latin. Speakers of Italian, German, English, etc., wrote in their own languages. Before this period, people spoke in a number of regional dialects and spellings were incredibly varied. With the new books, editors and authors began to make the first attempts at standardising spellings, grammar and other aspects of languages.

▲ An 18th-century illustration of Prince Hamlet startled by his father's ghost, from the famous opening act of Shakespeare's play Hamlet

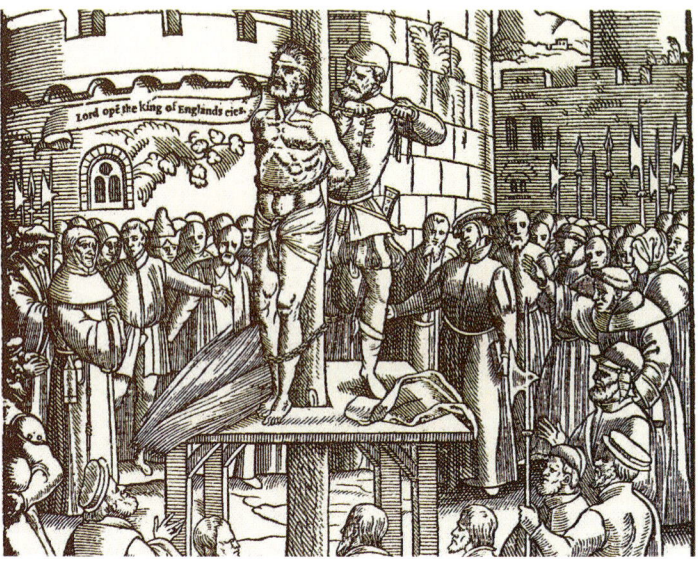

▲ William Tyndale, who published the first English translation of the Bible, was strangled, and then burnt on the orders of King Henry VIII; a 1563 woodcut from the Book of Martyrs by Protestant historian John Foxe

Vernacular Literature

In 1400, there was no standard form of English, French, German, Portuguese, Spanish or Italian. But as Renaissance authors wrote and published their books, editors and officials began to adopt the masterpieces as the basis for their national language. Martin Luther's German translation of the *Bible* in the early 16th century sold over half-a-million copies in that century. This is simply amazing, given that most people in that age didn't know how to read! Luther's East Middle-Saxon manner eventually became standard German. Italian was largely founded on the works of three authors—the poet Dante (1265–1321), the philosopher Petrarch, and the Humanist writer Boccaccio (1313–1375). Sixteenth-century writers adopted their Tuscan way of writing for all of Italy. William Tyndale's English *Bible*, the 1611 King James's *Bible* and William Shakespeare's masterful works deeply influenced English writers. Spain adopted the Castilian style after Miguel de Cervantes (1547–1616) published his brilliant book *Don Quixote*.

◄ The reconstructed Globe Theatre; William Shakespeare built the original in 1599 to stage his plays

▶ Our phrase 'tilting at windmills', meaning 'attacking imaginary enemies', comes from the scene of the misguided Don Quixote tilting (fighting) at windmills, imagining them to be fierce giants!

▲ Dante Alighieri

▲ Francesco Petrarch

▲ Giovanni Boccaccio

Music

Around 1330, an Italian school of music developed in northern cities of the region. This included Padua, Verona, Bologna, Florence and Milan. The verses were often in Italian. Leading composers such as Leonardo Giustiniani (1398–1446) and Marsilio Ficino would make up words as someone played the lute. Such experiments led to the invention of *contrapuntal* music—music that hinged on the pleasing interplay of two melodic lines. The Flemish composer Josquin Desprez (c. 1440–1521) was considered the greatest of the age. He wrote masses, **chansons** and **motets**. The works of Giovanni Pierluigi Palestrina (c. 1525–1594) and Orlando di Lasso (1532–1594) represent the zenith of Renaissance music.

▶ *Palestrina presenting his masses to Pope Julius III, a woodcut from 1554*

The Madrigal

The Renaissance saw the development of a special kind of song called the Madrigal. It was sung by small groups of people. Each person would carry a different part in the song. Occasionally, the lines would be played by an instrument. Madrigals were adored across Europe. By far the most popular one was *The White and Gentle Swan* by the Flemish composer Jacob Arcadelt. English composers who excelled at the madrigal included Thomas Weelkes, William Byrd, Thomas Morley and Orlando Gibbons. The most accomplished Italian madrigal composer was Claudio Monteverdi, who also developed the first major operas.

◀ *A portrait of Monteverdi by Bernardo Strozzi*

◀ *Cardinal Pietro Bembo (seen here in Titian's painting) was a great advocate of the Italian language, which led in part to the rise of the madrigal*

Sculpture

Italian sculptors of the Renaissance were often multi-talented, working as smiths and carvers of a variety of materials. The period is often taken to begin with the famous competition for the doors of the Florence Baptistery in 1403.

▲ The brilliant late-Renaissance sculptor Benvenuto Cellini (1500–1571) created Perseus with the head of Medusa, one of the masterpieces of 16th-century Florentine art

▲ The hugely influential Flemish genius Giambologna (1524–1608) specialised in bringing Classical stories to life, as with Hercules and Nessus (seen here) and Samson Slaying the Philistine

Lorenzo Ghiberti (1378–1455)

The son of a goldsmith, Lorenzo Ghiberti is best known for the Florence **baptistery's** eastern doors, named the 'Gates of Paradise' by Michelangelo. Each door is carved with five scenes from the Old Testament. Ghiberti used a painter's point of view to give the illusion of depth to each panel carving. He stressed on that illusion by having the figures closer to the viewer rounding outwards. In contrast, figures in the background appear to lie flat. This unusual perspective made figures less distinct, giving one the feeling that they were far away from the viewer.

▲ Panels on Ghiberti's Gates of Paradise

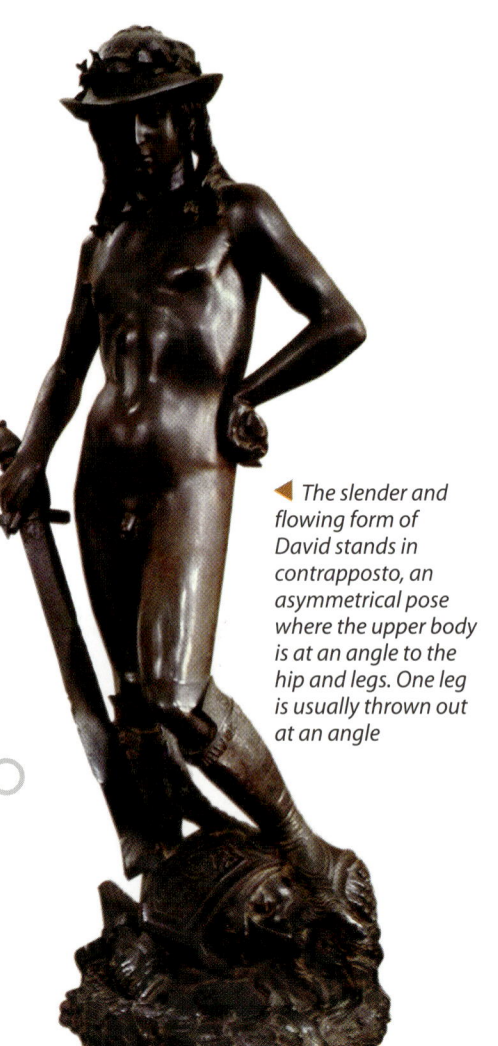

◄ The slender and flowing form of David stands in contrapposto, an asymmetrical pose where the upper body is at an angle to the hip and legs. One leg is usually thrown out at an angle

Donatello (c. 1386–1466)

A student of Brunelleschi's and an early assistant to Ghiberti, Donato di Niccolo di Betto Bardi (Donatello) was a master sculptor of early Renaissance. His workshop in Florence hosted many students. Donatello was inspired by Classical sculpture and expressed himself in stone, bronze, wood, clay, wax and **stucco**. He is considered the first Renaissance sculptor to celebrate the human body. His most famous work is the amazing life-size figure of David—the first-known free-standing nude statue made in Western Europe since ancient times.

Michelangelo (1475–1564)

The brilliant Michelangelo expressed his talent by painting and designing buildings. But it is his awe-inspiring sculptures that leave the greatest impression on the viewer. These are works of immense muscular power and profound emotion. Like Donatello, Michelangelo was enraptured by the human form and took pains to study it. An early example can be seen in his *Battle of the Centaurs*, which shows a multi-dimensional tangle of writhing bodies. In the more mature *Pieta*, he uses multiple contrasts to enhance the drama and pathos of Virgin Mary holding her dead son. A masterpiece of the same period is his heroic, gigantic *David*. Michelangelo's most refined style is seen in the *Moses* he created for the tomb of Pope Julius II.

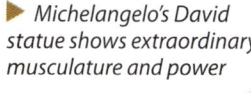

▶ *Michelangelo's David statue shows extraordinary musculature and power*

▲ *The unfinished Battle of the Centaurs (1492)*

▶ *Michelangelo moulded the Pieta (1498–1499) to show various contrasts—man and woman, vertical and horizontal, dead and alive, clothed and bare*

French Sculpture

Renaissance influence was first seen in French sculpture in Tours. Its main proponent was the amazing Michel Colombe (1432–1515). His 1508 relief sculpture of St. George and the Dragon was made for the high altar of the Chateau de Gaillon. It blends a Gothic theme with Italian modelling. Under Queen Catherine de'Medici (1519–1589), the royal house of France brought greater Italian influence into French art. The three great sculptors of this time were Pierre Bontemps (c. 1505–1568), Jean Goujon (c. 1510–c. 1568) and Germain Pilon (1535–1590).

▶ *Relief sculpture of nymphs by Jean Goujon at a fountain in Paris called Fontaine des Innocents*

Spanish Sculpture

The period 1530–1570 marked the zenith of Spanish Renaissance sculpture. This era was led by the amazing Alonso Berruguete (1488–1561) whose works show deep, religious emotions. Berruguete was a student of Michelangelo's. His most important works are the **retable** of the Mejorada, the retable of San Benito de Valladolid, the choir-stall reliefs in Toledo Cathedral and the fantastic tomb of Cardinal Tavera.

▶ *The retable of San Benito de Valladolid*

Architecture

Renaissance architects of Italy revived Classical Roman and Greek designs for buildings. Classicism focussed on set ideas of harmony, symmetry and proportion in all structures, whether it was a single building or an entire city. The earliest innovators of Renaissance architecture were engineers like Filippo Brunelleschi who worked in Florence. High Renaissance found its home in Rome, with geniuses like Donato Bramante, who served as chief architect in the construction of St Peter's Basilica. Over the 15th and 16th centuries, Renaissance architecture spread to the rest of Europe, where it combined with native styles to produce entirely unique buildings.

▲ *The Ideal City*, painted c. 1480–1484, depicts the ideal Renaissance town with its triumphant archway, Roman colosseum and octagonal baptistery surrounded by dignified homes. The entire space is broken up according to mathematical principles

Identifying Renaissance Architecture

Renaissance architecture followed mathematically calculated rules of geometry and proportion. On the outside, buildings looked austerely beautiful with repeated rows of columns and round arches, blind arches, medallions and sometimes, even statues. Three types of Classical columns—Doric, Ionic and Corinthian—were popular. Statues were used to decorate nooks and rooftops. Town plans radiated from a central point that had important buildings like a baptistery and **colosseum**.

◄ The Doric, Ionic and Corinthian styles for columns; the styles could be mixed to make composite columns

▶ Repeating rows of arches and columns topped by statues at the National Library of St Mark, designed by Renaissance architect Jacopo Sansovino

Filippo Brunelleschi (1377–1446)

A talented and technically skilled architect, Brunelleschi is best known for his amazing dome at the Duomo di Firenze (Cathedral of Florence). It is the first octagonal dome in history. Brunelleschi invented some of the machines that helped construct the dome! Brunelleschi is also famous for re-inventing the rules of perspective, which allowed artists to realistically portray three-dimensional spaces and objects on flat, two-dimensional paper.

▶ Cathedral of Florence with Brunelleschi's octagonal dome and Giotto's harmonious campanile (bell tower)

Grand Country Homes

Many wealthy Renaissance families ruled their lands from villas on vast country estates with beautifully designed gardens. The fabulous Villa d'Este is one such estate in Tivoli. It has playfully exaggerated, late-Renaissance (Mannerist) buildings; innumerable grand fountains; and terraced gardens that overlook the city of Florence. The architect Pirro Ligorio created it for Cardinal Ippolito II d'Este. The villa's famous gardens are set on a steep slope of the Sabine hills. A river plunges down the slope. Its waters are channelled into a spectacular variety of water features, including the remarkable 'water organ'. The stream runs around the garden, ostentatiously creating a forceful, theatrical effect.

▶ Fountain and garden at Villa d'Este, Tivoli

Donato Bramante (c. 1444–1514)

One of the masters of the Italian High Renaissance, Bramante brought the unique architecture to Rome when, under orders from Pope Julius II, he designed the Tempietto (small temple) of San Pietro in 1502. Surrounded by slender columns and mounted by a dome, the small building is almost like a sculpture. Yet, it has all the grandeur and correct proportions of Classical construction. Within a year of its completion, the impressed Pope asked Bramante to undertake the grandest architectural work of 16th-century Europe—the complete rebuilding of St Peter's Basilica.

▲ Commissioned by Ferdinand and Isabella of Spain, the Tempietto marks the spot in Rome where, according to legend, Saint Peter was crucified

▶ The amazing dome of St Peter's Basilica in Rome was created by Michelangelo

Science and Technology

After the dogma and superstition of the Middle Ages, Western Europe opened its mind to science once more during the Renaissance. This was caused by the rise of Humanism, the discovery of new lands and increased trade. The increase in exploration and commerce brought in the knowledge of the Islamic East and also revived an interest in Classical scholarship. In this fertile soil, the seeds of scientific investigation were first planted. The increasing use of gunpowder in wars fuelled technologies in both offence and defence. These went on to have wide-ranging applications in all walks of life.

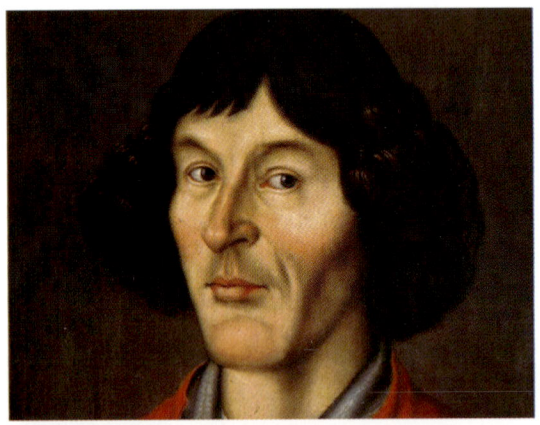

▲ Mathematician and astronomer Nicolaus Copernicus (1473–1543) put forth the theory of Heliocentrism, the idea that the Sun, not the Earth, was at the centre of the universe

▲ The Danish astronomer Tycho Brahe (1546–1601) observed the night sky before the telescope was invented. His studies of a comet and a supernova showed that the universe beyond the solar system was not as unchanging as was popularly believed

▲ English physician William Harvey (1578–1657) was the first man to describe our circulatory system in detail. He showed how blood was pumped by the heart to the brain and the body

Galileo Galilei (1564–1642)

A mathematician and astronomer, Galileo questioned a great many things that people took for granted as the work of God—like the occurrence of tides, the mechanics of objects in motion and the movement of heavenly bodies. He pioneered many practical tools of science, like the telescope. His telescopic observations gave the first verifiable evidence in support of Heliocentrism (*see p. 7*). In 1610, Galileo discovered the four largest moons of Jupiter. He named them in honour of four Medici brothers, one of whom—Grand Duke Cosimo II—later became his patron.

▲ Galileo was tried and condemned for heresy by the Inquisition for his support of Heliocentrism

▲ Galileo shows the Doge (duke) of Venice how to use a telescope

◀ As a child, Johannes Kepler (1571–1630) saw the Great Comet of 1577. He later formulated the laws of planetary motion that laid the foundation for Newton's discoveries on gravity

The Scientific Method

How is science conducted? The first real answer to this came during the Renaissance, when a method for science was set up. It was based on observation and gathering data. Do you have questions about the world around you? For instance, "Why is chocolate sweet?" A scientist would observe what goes into making chocolates and theorise that 'chocolate is sweet because of one or more of its ingredients'. He would test his theory—in this case, by tasting all the ingredients. The test would tell him that sugar in chocolate is sweet. Based on this result, the theory would be modified to reflect that newfound truth—that 'chocolate is sweet because it has sugar'. Most importantly in science, other people should be able to test a theory. If they come to the same conclusion that you did, then you gave a good, strong theory that many people will accept as truth.

▶ The English statesman Francis Bacon (1561–1626), one of the greatest Renaissance thinkers, developed the investigative method of science. It is named the Baconian Method in his honour

Leonardo da Vinci

Though he is best known for his paintings, Leonardo da Vinci was first and foremost a scientific mind. He observed and drew thousands of figures from nature, including details of human and horse anatomy. His discoveries extend into the field of acoustics and geology. He experimented with water flow, medical dissection, mechanics and aerodynamics. Da Vinci was even hired to engineer cannons, bridges, siege engines and defensive fortifications.

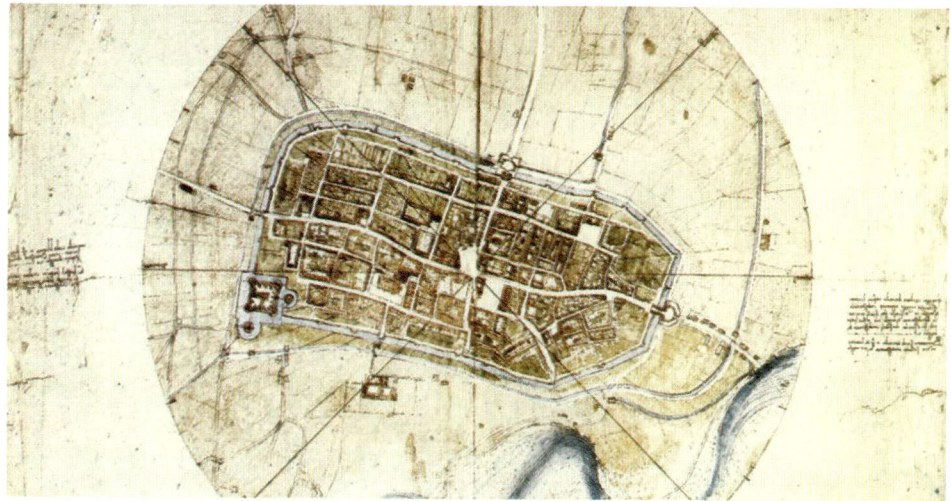

▲ Da Vinci created a coloured map of Imola as part of his plans to fortify the town. This is one of the earliest examples of a city map, drawn from a bird's-eye view

▲ In the 1470s, Renaissance Italy gave us the earliest-known parachute design. Around 1485, Leonardo da Vinci took it a step further. The Venetian inventor Fausto Veranzio (1551–1617) further modified da Vinci's parachute sketch with a bulging sail-like piece of cloth (as seen here) that was more effective at slowing down a fall

The Printing Press

The spread of knowledge during the Renaissance was fuelled by the invention of the moveable printing press by the German goldsmith, Johannes Gutenberg (1398–1468). The mechanical device could produce 3,600 pages in a working day. No longer were books luxury items that had to be laboriously copied by hand. By the start of the 16th century, over 200 European cities had printing presses. People could now read the *Bible* in their own language. They became aware of the corruption in the Catholic Church. This fuelled the Protestant Reformation (*see pp. 22–23*).

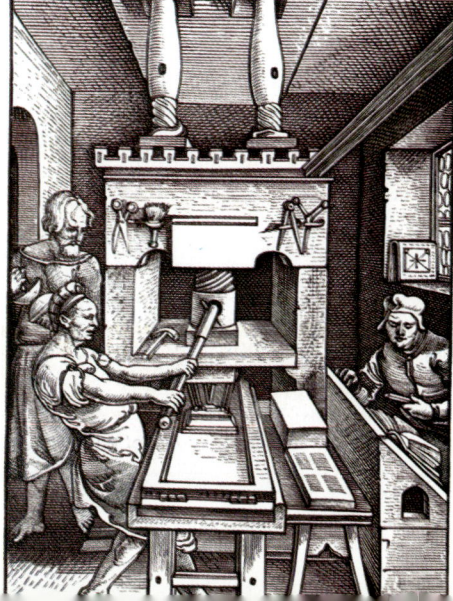

▶ The printing press, arguably the single most influential event of the Renaissance

Exploration and Reformation

The Renaissance coincided with two other European phenomena: the Age of Exploration (roughly 1450–1600) and the Reformation Period. The former refers to the European discovery of the Americas and of new trade routes to Africa and Asia. Great strides were made in navigational tools, ship technologies and map-making. At the same time, a great religious and political upheaval took place at home. Led by the German monk Martin Luther, this was called the Protestant Reformation. The Catholic Church ceased to be the sole form of Christianity in the West.

▲ The map of the world as given by 2nd-century-BCE Roman mathematician and astronomer Ptolemy was finally discarded during the Age of Discovery! New and increasingly accurate maps were made during the 15th–17th centuries

1415
The Portuguese seize the Muslim port-city of Ceuta in northern Africa. This inspires Prince Henry—known as Henry the Navigator—to initiate the Age of Discovery with explorations of trade routes along West Africa.

1492
Christopher Columbus lands in the Caribbean. He misguidedly believes it to be Asia and claims it for the Spanish crown!

1497
Under the banner of Henry VII of England, Italian adventurer John Cabot lands on the east coast of North America. He too mistakes it for Asia and claims it for England!

1498
Vasco da Gama reaches India by rounding the tip of Africa, thus discovering a new route to Asia.

▶ Vasco da Gama lands at Calicut, India; c. 1880 by Ernesto Casanova

1509
The Portuguese win the Battle of Diu against an alliance of the Sultan of Gujarat, the Mamluk Sultan of Egypt and the Zamorin of Calicut, marking the start of Portugal's dominance of the Indian Ocean spice trade.

1600
English merchants found the East India Company and set out to exploit trade in Asia and India.

1562–98
The French Wars of Religion take place between Catholics and Huguenots (French Protestants) and end when Henry IV grants religious rights in the Edict of Nantes.

◀ This painting by the Huguenot Francois Dubois depicts the 1572 St Bartholomew's Day Massacre in which Catholic mobs slaughtered thousands of their Protestant countrymen. The massacre went on for weeks!

1558
Queen Elizabeth I restores religious tolerance in England.

1554
Queen Mary enforces Catholicism in England, executing and burning her subjects for heresy. They name her Bloody Mary.

1545–63
At the Council of Trent, the Catholic Church puts Counter-Reformation activities into motion to counter the Protestant movement.

◀ The Council of Trent, 1588, by Italian painter Pasquale Cati

WORLD HISTORY | RENAISSANCE

▲ The church doors on which Luther posted his reforms were destroyed in a fire. In 1857, King Frederick William IV of Prussia ordered their replacement. Luther's words are now engraved into this door

Martin Luther posts his 95 Theses on the door of a church in Wittenburg, Germany, igniting the Protestant Reformation.

◀ Map of the island city Tenochtitlan and the Mexican gulf, made by one of Cortes's men

Spanish **conquistador** Hernan Cortes's horrific assault on the Aztec capital of Tenochtitlan inspires other Europeans to conquer the Americas.

1509–11
The most influential Dutch humanist Desiderius Erasmus (1466–1536) publishes *In Praise of Folly*—an attack on European orthodoxy and superstitions.

1517

1519
Explorer Ferdinand Magellan sets out to journey around the world. Three years later, his ship *Vittoria* completes the first circumnavigation of the globe.

1521
Luther appears at the **Diet** of Worms before Charles V, Holy Roman Emperor, on charges of heresy. He is excommunicated by Pope Leo X.

▶ Luther at the diet (imperial council) in the city of Worms

Henry VIII separates the Church of England from the Catholic Church of Rome.

1541
Francisco de Orellana encounters and explores the Amazon River.

1534
Francisco Pizarro leads the Spanish conquest of the Incan Empire.

1532

1526
William Tyndale publishes the English *Bible*.

1522
Luther begins translating the *Bible* into German. For the first time, ordinary Germans can read the word of God.

◀ In 1533, Pizarro executes the last Incan emperor

Islamic Eurasia

At the start of the Renaissance, Muslim lands were prosperous. The major Islamic empires had become more centralised. The Ottomans controlled vast domains in southeastern Europe, Turkey, northwest Africa, Egypt and Syria; and the Safavids ruled Iran and Iraq. By the end of the period, however, these empires were rapidly shrinking and giving way to Western expansion and colonisation.

Ottoman Empire

In 1453, Sultan Mehmet II captured Constantinople. Renaming it Istanbul, he turned the city into the Ottoman capital. It became the seat of one of the most powerful empires ever seen. Ottoman territory and culture reached its height under the rule of Suleiman the Magnificent (ruled 1520–1566). His people called him the Lawgiver. He sent governors—called Pashas or Beys—to rule the many nations that came under Ottoman sway.

▲ The Timurid Empire stretched beyond Persia, modern Afghanistan and Central Asia. However, it shrunk rapidly after the death of its founder, Timur, in 1405. By the early 16th century, the original empire was extinct

▲ Francis I and Suleiman the Magnificent agree to a Franco-Ottoman alliance; c. 1530, believed to be painted by Titian

The Safavid Empire

The Safavids were rulers of Persia (Iran) over the 14th–18th centuries. The state was founded not by warriors but by a medieval holy man named Shaykh Safi al-Din (c. 1252–1334). At the start of the 16th century, his followers defeated the rulers of northern Iran. Their teenage leader Ismail I (ruled 1501–1524) proclaimed himself Shah, using the ancient title for Persian rulers. Ismail united all of Iran for the first time since the 7th century! The Safavids fought with the Ottomans for the fertile plains of Iraq. The warring lasted for more than 150 years and Baghdad changed hands numerous times.

▶ The Safavid's most notable ruler was Shah Abbas I (1571–1629). Europeans were amazed by his capital city of Isfahan, with its innumerable parks, libraries, schools, shops and public baths

Incredible Individuals

Suleiman's favourite wife, Hurrem Sultan, rose from being a slave to the most influential woman of the empire. She took an active part in state affairs, which was unheard of in that male-dominated world.

▲ Titian's c. 1550 painting titled La Sultana Rossa is thought to be a portrait of Hurrem Sultan

The Tsardom of Russia

Mongol power in Russian lands declined after a united army, led by Prince Dmitry Donskoy of Moscow (1350–89), defeated the Mongol-Tatars in the 1380 Battle of Kulikovo. Over the 15th century, Moscow absorbed neighbouring states such as Tver and Novgorod. Ivan III (1440–1505), dubbed the Great, finally brought all of central and northern Rus under Moscow's control. He became the first Grand Duke of Russia. His grandson, the infamous Ivan the Terrible, took complete hold of the **boyars** and Russian territories. In 1547, he was crowned the first Tsar ('Caesar') of Russia.

▲ A 19th-century painting at the Grand Kremlin Palace, Moscow, shows Prince Dmitry Donskoy in the Battle of Kulikovo

Ivan the Terrible (1530–84)

The nickname 'Terrible' meant terrifying and awe-inspiring. The early part of Ivan's rule was marked by glorious leadership. Later in life, he descended into madness and became a cruel despot. Over his life, Ivan nearly doubled the size of Russia. He introduced the printing press, revised the laws, limited the power of the Church and created a standing army. He encouraged the expansion of trade, making Russia rich and multicultural. But after the death of his beloved wife, Ivan became sick and disabled. His secret service network—the Oprichnina—became increasingly ruthless, murdering thousands of people to satisfy the paranoid and unbalanced monarch. On his death, Ivan left behind a ravaged nation, a broken government and an unfit heir.

▲ In a fit of maniacal rage, Ivan the Terrible killed his own son. Russian artist Ilya Repin painted a grief-stricken Tsar cradling his mortally wounded son. Ivan's other son, who inherited the throne, was mentally unfit to rule

From Rurik to Romanov

The death of Ivan's sons marked the end of the Rurik Dynasty in 1598. It was followed by the Time of Troubles, which saw severe famine and civil war. A number of pretenders tried to take the throne. This ended in 1613, when the council of ministers made Michael I Tsar. He established the Romanov Dynasty, the last royal family to rule Russia.

Isn't It Amazing!

Owing in part to the widespread, hygienic practice of banya—a wet steam bath—Russia suffered fewer losses during the plague outbreaks over 1350–1490 than the rest of Europe.

▲ A traditional banya, painted by Russian artist Tichov (1876–1939)

▲ Among the pretenders to the throne was False Dmitri I (ruled 1605–1606). His short rule ended when he was captured and killed by a mob of boyars

▲ Sixteen-year-old Michael is offered the crown at the Ipatiev Monastery in 1613

Mughal India

The Mughal Empire ruled great swathes of the Indian subcontinent from 1526–1858. At its height, in the early 18th century, the empire stretched over modern-day Afghanistan, Pakistan, Myanmar and almost all of India. The dynasty was founded by a descendent of Timur called Babur. In 1526, he defeated Sultan Ibrahim Lodi of Delhi at the First Battle of Panipat. This was the first time gunpowder was used in India. After his death, the empire went to his heirs, Humayun (1508–1556), Akbar (1543–1605), Jahangir (1569–1627), Shah Jahan (1592–1666), Aurangzeb (1618–1707) and then a series of increasingly powerless rulers.

Akbar the Great

By far the most charismatic and broad-minded Mughal ruler, Akbar the Great was enthroned when he was just 14 years old. The empire was on shaky ground at this time. Delhi itself had been conquered by a minister called Hemu. Akbar's armies met and defeated Hemu at the Second Battle of Panipat, securing the throne for the Mughal ruler. Akbar continued to expand his territory—first under the guidance of his chief minister Bairam Khan and after 1560, on his own. His military conquests gained him a sprawling empire that killed thousands. But he also tried to rule his subjects justly. He bridged religious barriers and supported scholarship and art. Stocky and only 5ft 7in tall, with a 'lucky' wart on his nose, Akbar was alert, physically tough and energetic. He could not read or write, but he loved art, poetry, debate, music and philosophy. He oversaw a golden age of Indian art and culture. Unfortunately, his enlightened policies were reversed under the rule of his great-grandson, Aurangzeb.

▲ *This c. 1811 painting shows Akbar the Great on the Peacock Throne, the legendary jewelled throne of the Mughal emperors that was actually commissioned later, in Shah Jahan's time*

▼ *The pinnacle of Mughal architecture, the Taj Mahal was built over 1630–1653 by Emperor Shah Jahan as a tomb for his beloved wife Mumtaz Mahal*

The Nine Gems

The court of Akbar the Great attracted numerous talents. Most famous among them were the group of men called the Nine Gems. Tansen (c.1500–1586) was a gifted singer who revolutionised classical music with his compositions. The wise and witty Birbal (1528–1583) was appointed to court as a favoured counsellor and eventually given the title Raja. Abul Fazl (1551–1602) was Akbar's historian. Over many years, he painstakingly documented the monarch's life and rule in the amazing book, *Akbarnama*. The poet Faizi (1547–1595) was a genius at composing Persian verse. He became most famous for his translation of a 12th-century book on mathematics called *Lilavati*. Akbar made him tutor to his son. Todar Mal handled the empire's finances as its *diwan*. He introduced standard weights and measures, and created a systematic approach to revenue collection. Man Singh, the Raja of Amber, was Akbar's trusted lieutenant in many successful campaigns. The poet Abdul Rahim Khan-I-Khan was the son of Bairam Khan. Fagir Aziao Din and Mullan Do Piaza were two other important advisors.

▶ *Raja Birbal, a 19th-century painting*

▲ *Akbar receives the poet Abdul Rahim Khan-I-Khan, son of Bairam Khan*

▲ *Abul Fazl presents the Akbarnama to Emperor Akbar*

Religion

Under Akbar, religious tolerance became the norm. The *jizya*—a tax on non-Muslims—was dropped. The Muslim lunar calendar gave way to the more practical solar calendar. Akbar even developed a religion by mixing the best of Hinduism, Islam and Christianity. He called it Din-i-Ilahi. His descendant Aurangzeb, however, was a devout Muslim who imposed Islamic law and treated his non-Muslim subjects harshly. In response to the strong Islamic presence, Hinduism experienced a resurgence, called the Bhakti movement. At the same time, a new religion called Sikhism was founded by Guru Nanak.

▶ *Guru Nanak (1469–1539)*

▶ *Babur and his followers visit a Hindu temple, an illustration from the emperor's biography Baburnama*

Imperial China

At the start of the 15th century, the Ming Dynasty ruled China. The Yongle Emperor (1360–1424) put down his rivals and solidified his power, both in court and with neighbouring states. He lay down the foundations for the fabulous imperial residence, the Forbidden City. Literature and art blossomed in Beijing. China funded far-flung naval explorations. The exquisite blue-and-white Ming porcelain became a highly sought-after treasure. Eventually, corruption and infighting brought down the Ming Empire. Rebellions broke out across the land. When an army of Manchus invaded, the Ming could not repel them. In 1644, the Manchus set up the Qing Dynasty—the last imperial dynasty of China.

▲ A blue-and-white Ming-period dish painted with a dragon

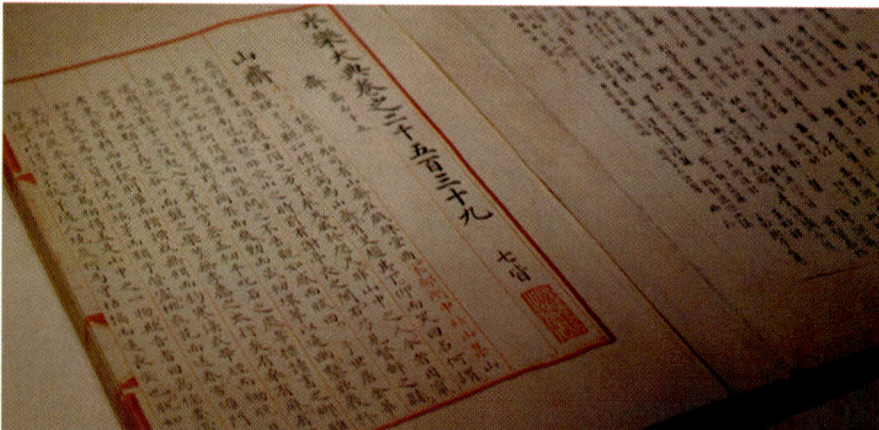

▲ The Yongle Dadian was a massive encyclopedia—22,000 chapters long! It is one of the most important Chinese literary works from the time of Emperor Yongle. Sadly, only some 800 chapters remain today

Engineering an Empire

In the early 15th century, the Mongols rose briefly to harass China's borders. In response, Emperor Yongle moved his capital to the more defensible city of Beijing in 1421. He spent a great deal enlarging the city and securing it with a 10-m-high wall that ran around Beijing for 15 km! To meet the new city's food demands, he rebuilt the Grand Canal, so grain ships could reach the capital. He also repaired the Great Wall of China to strengthen the northern borders.

▲ The Zijincheng (Purple Forbidden City) covers 7.2 km² and has thousands of rooms, carefully laid out according to the traditional Chinese view of the world. There is even a river running through the estate. At the heart of the complex, on the most elevated site, is the Hall of Supreme Harmony, where imperial receptions were held

In Real Life

Like many governments today, Ming China was run by civil servants. A job with the civil service was highly coveted. Applicants sat for difficult exams. The men who scored the highest got the best jobs. Men studied for years to pass the exam and earn a prestigious position.

▶ Civil-service candidates waiting for their results, c. 1540, by Qiu Ying

Women in Ming China

The stability and increased wealth of the Ming period led to a sharp rise in the population. As cities grew, women from the richer families began to gain more freedom. They owned businesses in their own name and could trade as merchants. They were even allowed to be professional artists. Sadly, other laws—such as a widow's right to inherit her husband's property—were lost at this time. Indeed, widows were expected to follow their husbands in death!

▶ By the Ming period, young girls from all walks of life would have their feet tightly—and cruelly—bound to keep them small throughout their life. Special 'lotus shoes' like this Qing-period shoe were embroidered for feet, which were supposed to be no larger than 10 cm!

Isn't It Amazing!

Though he did much good for China, Yongle Emperor was also immensely cruel at times. On taking the throne, he killed most of the preceding emperor's servants. In another horrific event, he ordered 2,800 concubines, servant girls and guards to a slow-slicing death! His successor freed many of the survivors.

▲ Yongle Emperor on the Dragon chair

Zheng He (c. 1371–1433)

The greatest explorer of the period was the military general and diplomat Zheng He. A Muslim by birth, Zheng He was only 10 years old when he was forced to join the Ming army. He soon made powerful friends at court. When the emperor wanted to conquer the 'Western Oceans', he chose Zheng He to lead the navy. Zheng He undertook seven voyages—with hundreds of ships—and explored Asia, India, the Middle East and East Africa.

◀ After visiting Somalia in Africa, Zheng brought back a giraffe for Emperor Yongle!

Rise of the Qing Emperors

In 1644, a rebel army under the command of Li Zicheng (1605–1645) attacked Beijing. When it entered the city in April, the last Ming emperor—Chongzhen (ruled 1628–1644)—hung himself. An army commander called Wu Sangai heard this news while he was fighting Manchu troops in northeastern China. He quickly made peace with them and requested their help. The Manchus obliged. But once they had put down the rebellion, they decided to stay on as rulers! Li Zicheng was killed by peasants and the Manchus established the Qing Dynasty, which ruled for almost three centuries.

▲ Qing Dynasty's fourth monarch, the Kangxi Emperor (1654–1722), who completed the Manchu conquest of China

The Unification of Japan

At the start of the 15th century, Japanese states had an imperial figurehead but were actually ruled by military warlords (Shogun) of the Ashikaga family. The Shoguns of the first half of this period faced severe famines and civil war, which culminated in the Onin War (1467–1477). After this war, the local leaders *(daimyo)* of individual states became so powerful, they broke free from the Shogun's rule. Having so many military leaders led to a time of violence and disunity called the Sengoku—the Warring States Period. The men who unified Japan again were Oda Nobunaga and—after his death—Toyotomi Hideyoshi and Tokugawa Ieyasu. The Sengoku ended with the formation of the phenomenal Tokugawa Shogunate, which lasted until the late 19th century.

▲ *Oda Nobunaga watches a Sumo (wrestling) tournament*

▲ *The armour of Oda Nobunaga*

Oda Nobunaga (1534–1582)

From the bloody struggles of the Sengoku *daimyo* rose an unexpected leader. He was the head of a small province called Owari. No one expected Oda Nobunaga to become the powerful leader of Japan. Yet, he succeeded in occupying the capital. Oda was a military genius who successfully adapted firearms to Japanese warfare. He also developed military infrastructure like ironclad ships, a network of roads and formidable castles. His armies could thus move at great speed. Most importantly, Oda chose his warriors for their ability, not based on class, rank or family connections. He suppressed not only the other *daimyos* but also broke the power of warrior-monks. Oda was also a talented statesman, establishing economic and financial laws that made it easier for his people to live in tough times.

Honno-ji Temple

At the height of his power, Oda Nobunaga was betrayed by his general Akechi Mitsuhide. While Nobunaga was resting in a temple, he was surrounded by Mitsuhide and his troops. Nobunaga ordered his **page**, Mori Ranmaru, to set the temple on fire so no one could take his head. He then committed suicide. His devoted page followed soon after.

◄ *Oda displayed his power and prestige by supporting the arts and building amazing gardens and castles. His Azuchi castle on Lake Biwa was covered with gold statues on the outside, while the inside was decorated with exquisitely painted screens and ceilings*

🕒 The Hideyoshi Regime

Oda was betrayed just as he was poised to achieve his goal. His brilliant counsellor Toyotomi Hideyoshi (1537–98) took over the unification of Japan. The son of a peasant, Toyotomi rose to become one of Nobunaga's most powerful commanders. He eliminated many rivals (including the rebel Akechi Mitsuhide) using his shrewd judgment and prompt actions. By 1590, all Japan was in his control.

▶ *Known as the One-Eyed Dragon of Oshu, the daimyo Date Masamune (1567–1636) was an outstanding military tactician and man of high ethics in a time of war and unrest. He served both Toyotomi and Tokugawa and is venerated as a hero to this day*

▲ *Gazing up Toyotomi Hideyoshi's skinny, lined face, Oda Nobunaga nicknamed him Kozaru, meaning Little Monkey!*

🕒 The Tokugawa Shogunate

Because they were of relatively humble origin, neither Oda nor Hideyoshi took the title of Shogun. After Hideyoshi's death, another Oda ally, Tokugawa Ieyasu (1543–1616), won power at the 1600 Battle of Sekigahara. In 1603, he took the title of Shogun, establishing a period of peace and stability. The rule of his successors Hidetada and Iemitsu saw a rise in the persecution of Christians. Things came to a head in the Shimabara Rebellion of 1637–1638 during which thousands of Christian rebels and sympathisers were executed. Soon after, Japan expelled all foreigners and isolated itself from the world for the next 200+ years!

▲ *Tokugawa Ieyasu, founder of the last Shogunate of Japan*

⭐ Incredible Individuals

Toyotomi was a great supporter of tea master Sen no Rikyu (1552–1591), the man who took the Japanese tea ceremony to new heights. All current tea masters trace their lineage to him. Rikyu was, however, forced to commit *seppuku*—ritual suicide—in 1591, owing to Hideyoshi's actions.

▶ *The original tea-ceremony master Sen no Rikyu in a painting by the great artist Hasegawa Tohaku (1539–1610)*

▲ *Christian prisoners of the 17th century awaiting execution*

Word Check

Baptistery: This is the part of a church that is used for performing baptisms, a rite of passage for being accepted as a Christian.

Boyar: This is the term for Russian nobility.

Catholics: Christianity is divided into many groups that hold slightly differing beliefs. Catholics form the largest of these groups. They are guided by the Pope, the Bishop of Rome.

Chanson: This is a song with French words or a song whose words have been set to music by a French composer.

Chiaroscuro: This refers to the effect of contrasting light and shadow in an artwork.

City-state: A small territory, centred on a powerful city, that acts as an independent nation

Classical: In the context of scholarship and art, this refers to the knowledge and learning of Ancient Greece and Rome.

Colosseum: This refers to a large open theatre or stadium built by Ancient Romans

Condottieri: In medieval and Renaissance Italy, this referred to leaders of troops that fought for money (rather than out of loyalty for a country or cause)

Conquistador: The men who led the Spanish and Portuguese conquests of South America

Constantinople: Modern-day Istanbul in Turkey was the centre of the Eastern Roman Empire—or the Byzantine Empire—during the Middle Ages. The city was then called Constantinople, after the Roman Emperor Constantine the Great (c. 272–337 CE), who made it his capital city.

Diet: An imperial council; the Diet of Worms was held in the city of Worms.

El Greco: This is the nickname of Doménikos Theotokópoulos (1541–1614). His dramatic, twisted artworks were way ahead of their time and puzzled many of his contemporaries.

Epidemic: An epidemic is the widespread occurrence of infectious diseases at any given time.

Execution: This is the act of carrying out the death sentence on a person judged to be a criminal.

Fresco: This is the art of painting on a wall while its coating of plaster is still fresh and moist.

Marranos: Jews who converted to Christianity officially but still practised Judaism secretly

Motet: This refers to church music sung by a choir without using any instruments. The words are usually in Latin. If the words are in English, it is called an anthem.

New World: This refers to the Americas and many Pacific islands, which became prominent from the 16th century onwards, after Western explorers began to conquer it.

Old World: This refers to Africa, Asia and Europe, lands that have been known to humankind since ancient times.

Page: A young attendant, usually a boy

Perspective: This refers to the way in which three-dimensional objects are painted or sculpted so as to give a viewer different ideas/perceptions of height, width, depth and relative position.

Polymath: This refers to a person of great and varied learning.

Protestants: This refers to Christians who broke away from the Catholic Church in the 16th century. They believed Catholicism had become corrupt and sought a way back to the original teachings of Christianity.

Retable: This is a frame that holds carved or decorated panels. It is placed just behind the altar.

Sack of Rome: Sacking is the brutal pillaging of a town or city by an invading army. In the course of history, Rome has been sacked seven times!

Sfumato: This is an art technique that creates soft forms using gradually changing tones, shades and colours, rather than sharp, clear outlines.

Spanish Inquisition: This was a Roman Catholic court set up by Spain to root out any religious beliefs that were contrary to Catholicism.

Stucco: This is a fine plaster used inside buildings for decoration or ornamentation.

Tintoretto: This Italian painter lived over 1518–94. A master of the Venice school of art, he was hailed for both the speed of his painting and his powerful brushwork.

Treatise: A formal, written work that is a scholarly exploration of a subject

Triptych: This is an artwork that is spread over three panels.

Triumvirate: This refers to a group of three people holding power over a territory (instead of a single monarch). Ancient Rome of the 1st century BCE was sometimes ruled by a triumvirate of men.